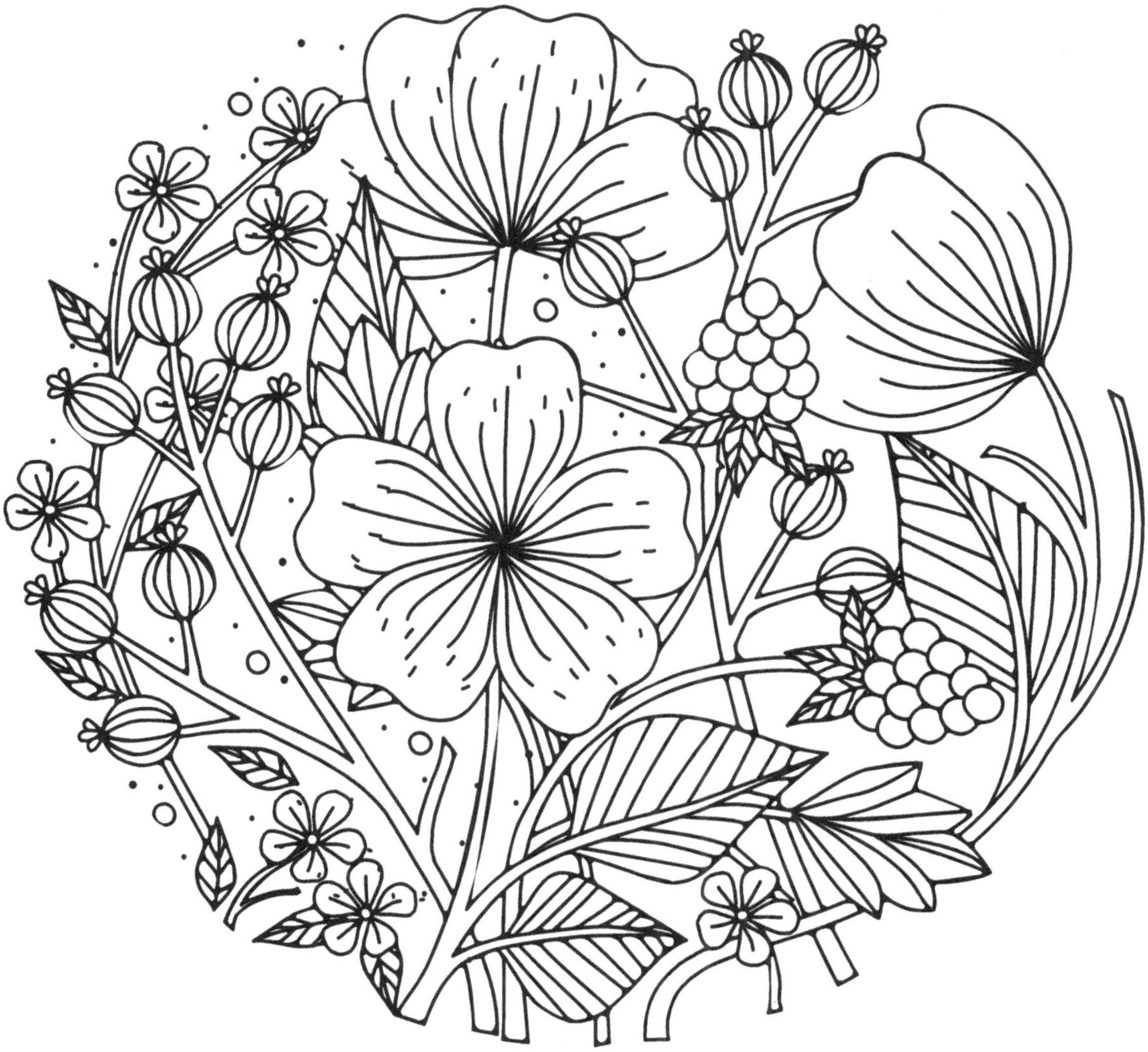

Pregnant
with triplets

by Naomi Dorland

Pregnant with Triplets: Mindful colouring for triplet pregnancy
ISBN: 978-0-6485846-1-2

First Published in 2021 in Australia

www.twinfo.com.au

First Printed in Australia: IngramSpark
Cover Design: Naomi Dorland
Colouring Pages: Naomi Dorland
Print Layout: Louise Addison, Radge Design

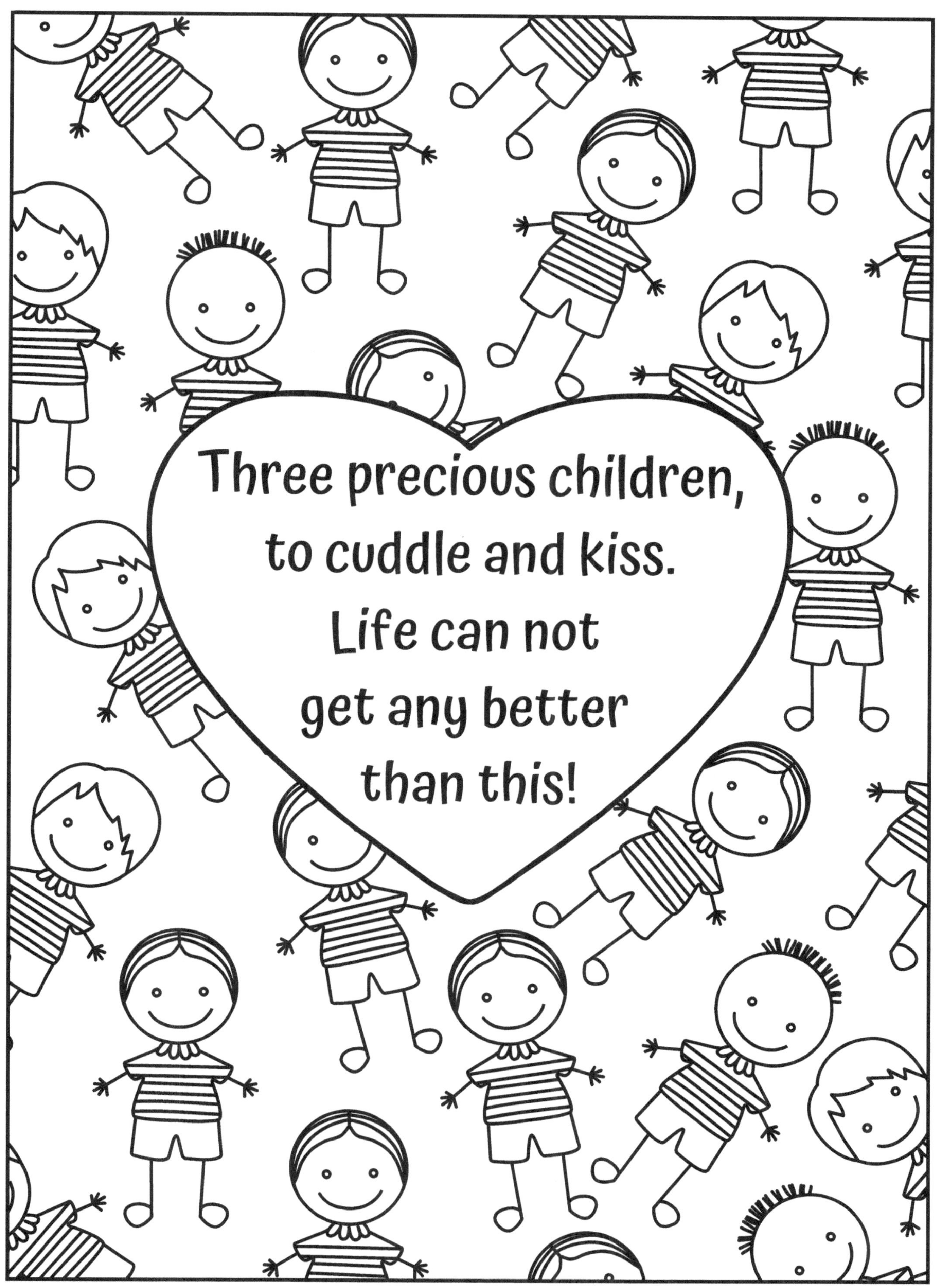Three precious children,
to cuddle and kiss.
Life can not
get any better
than this!

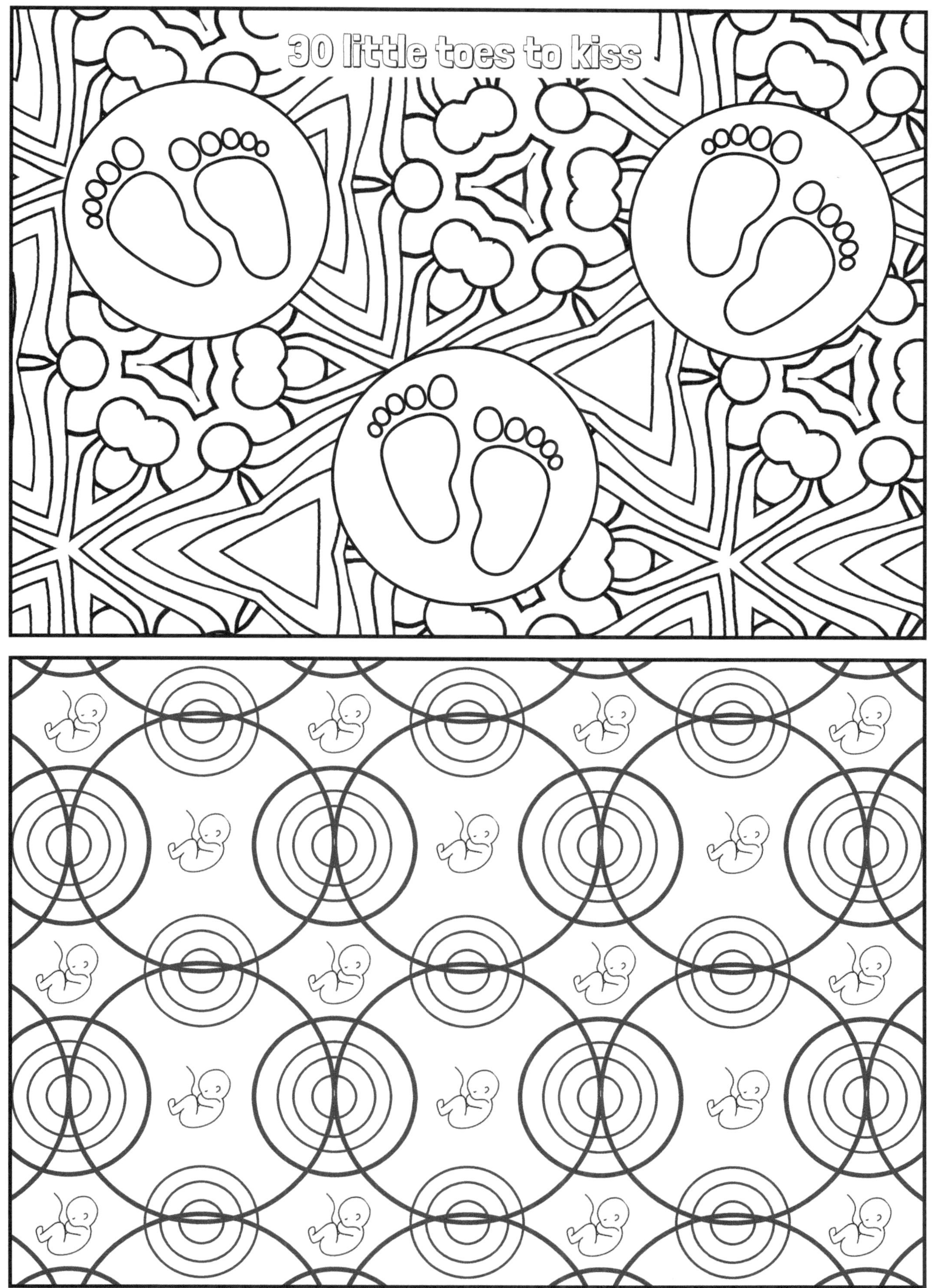
30 little toes to kiss

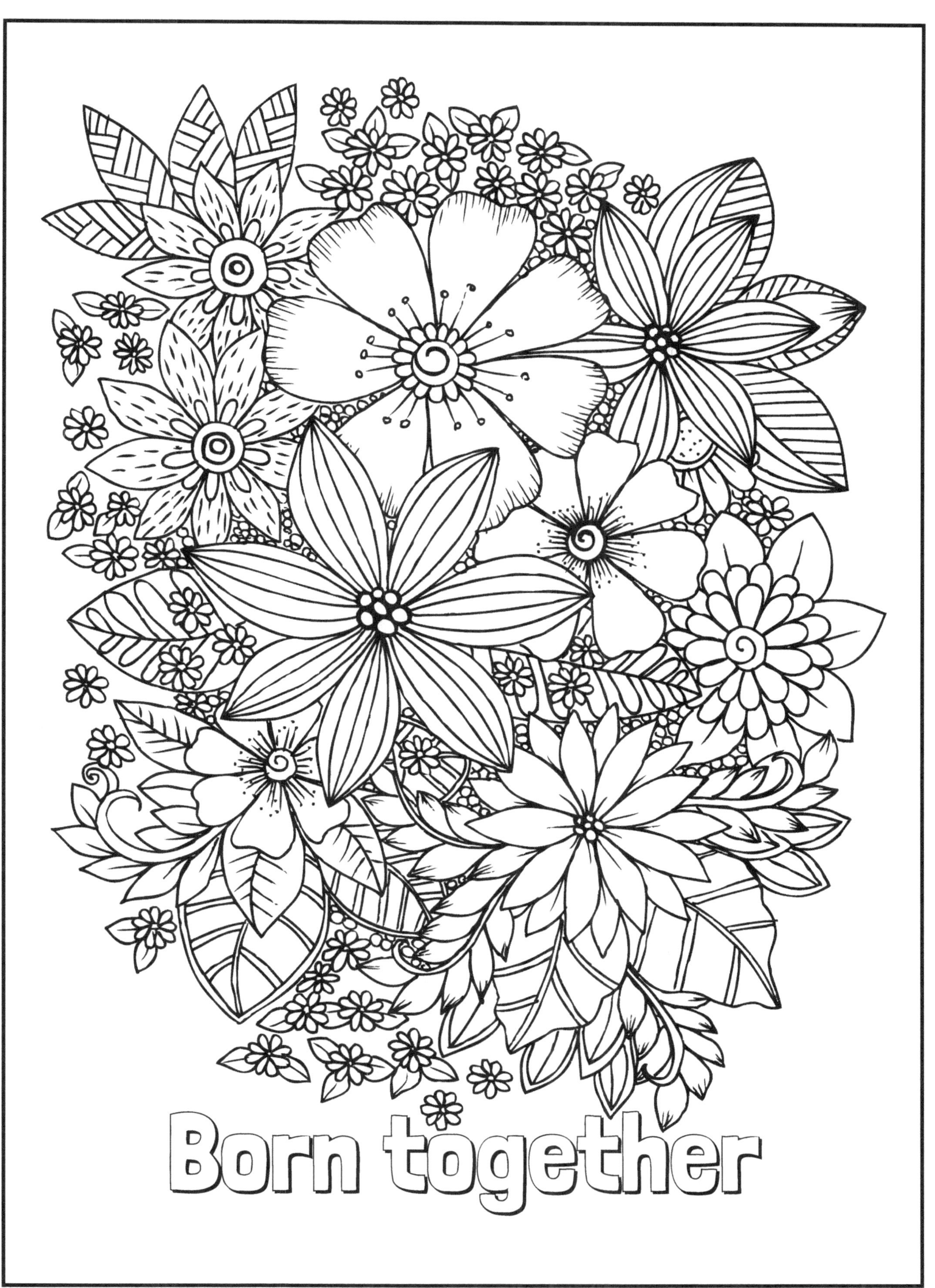

Born together

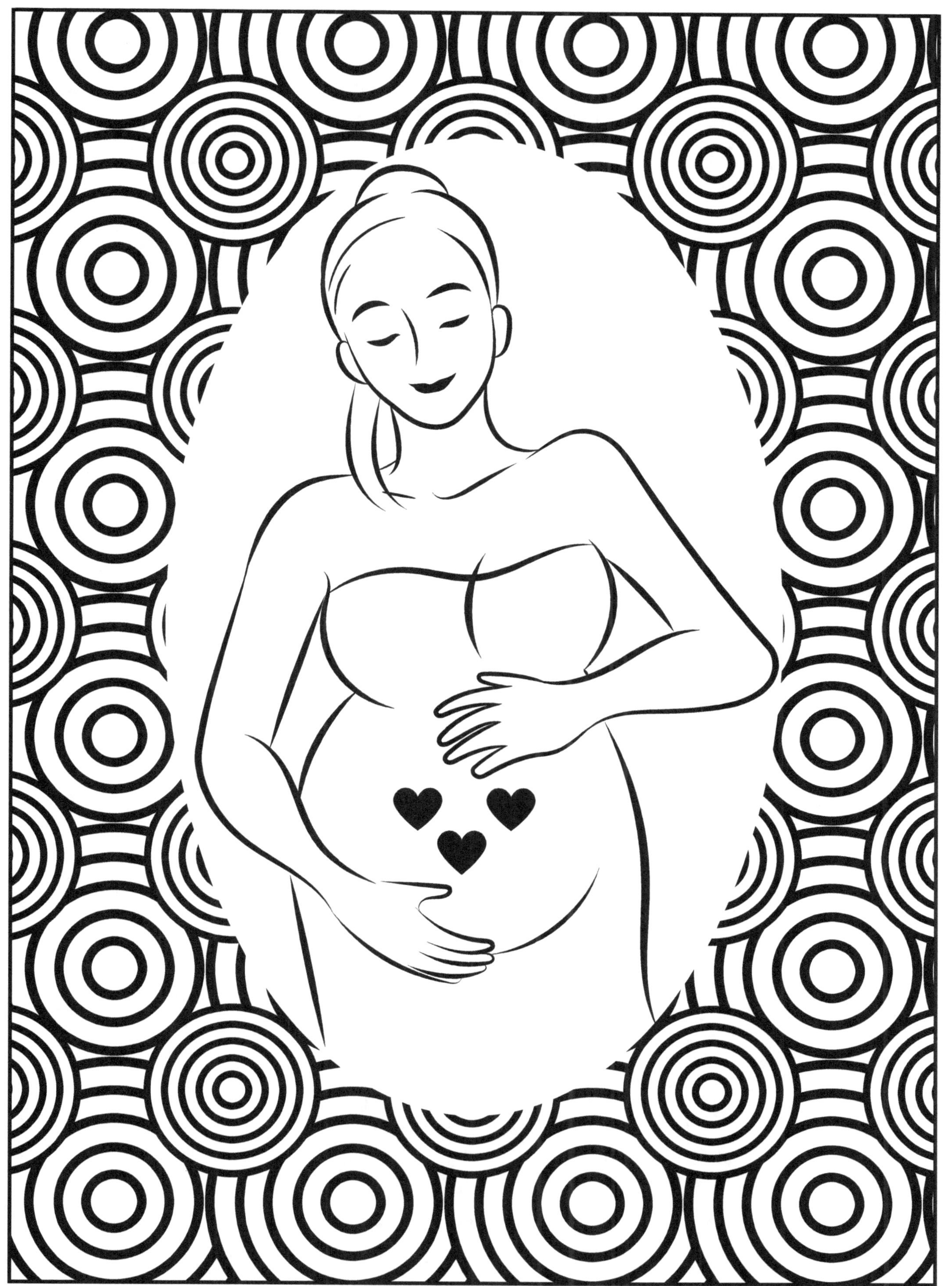

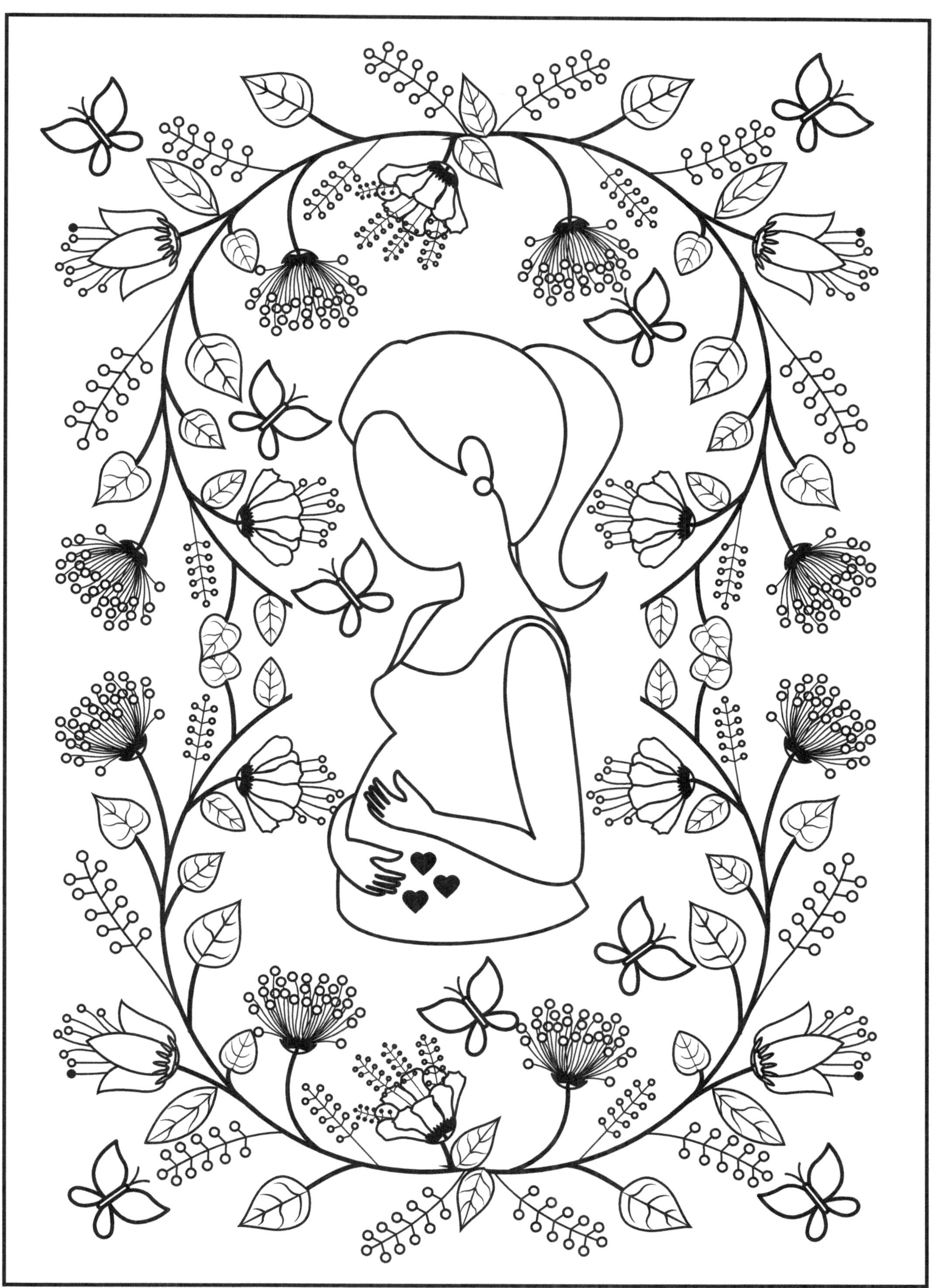

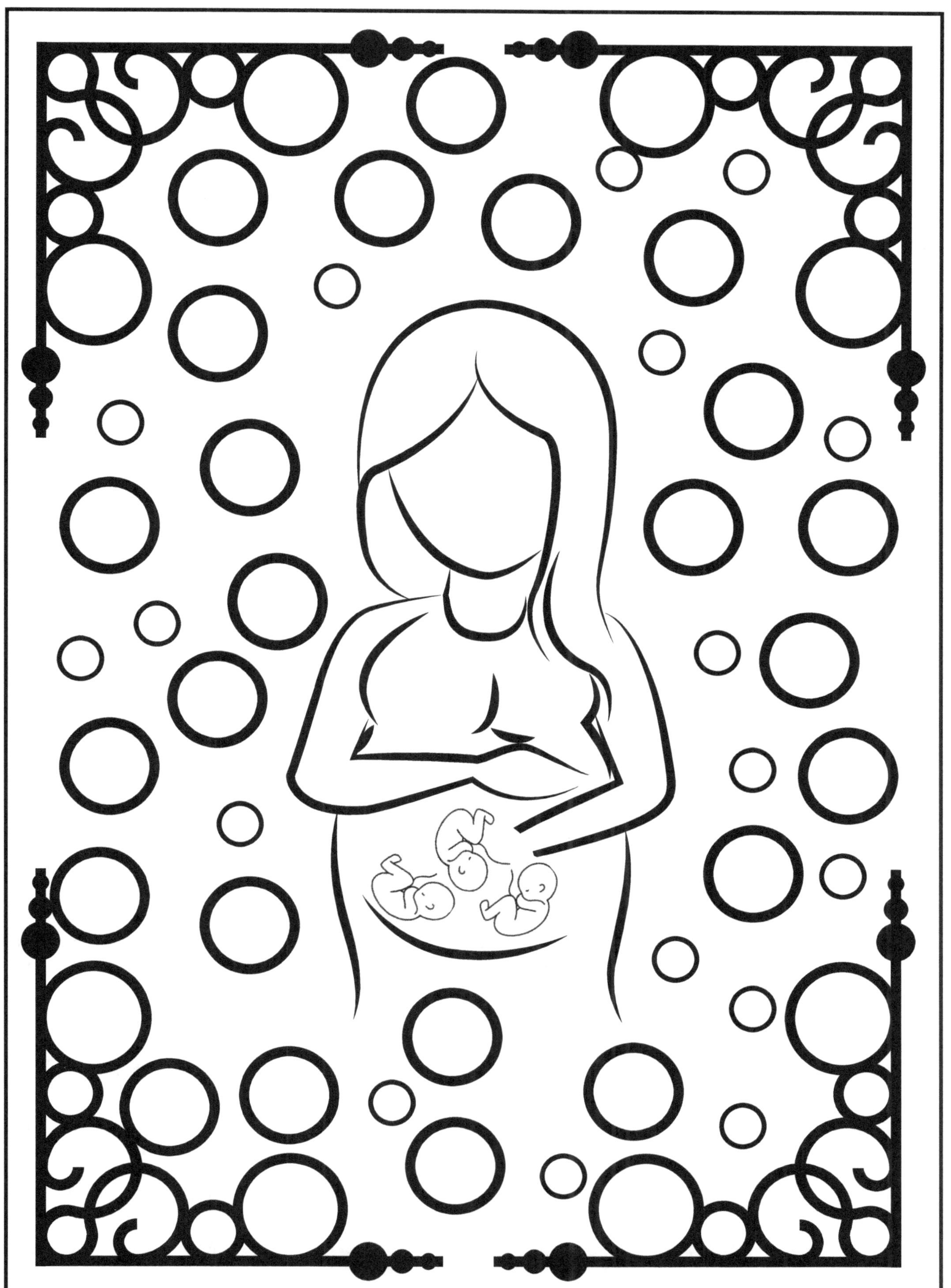

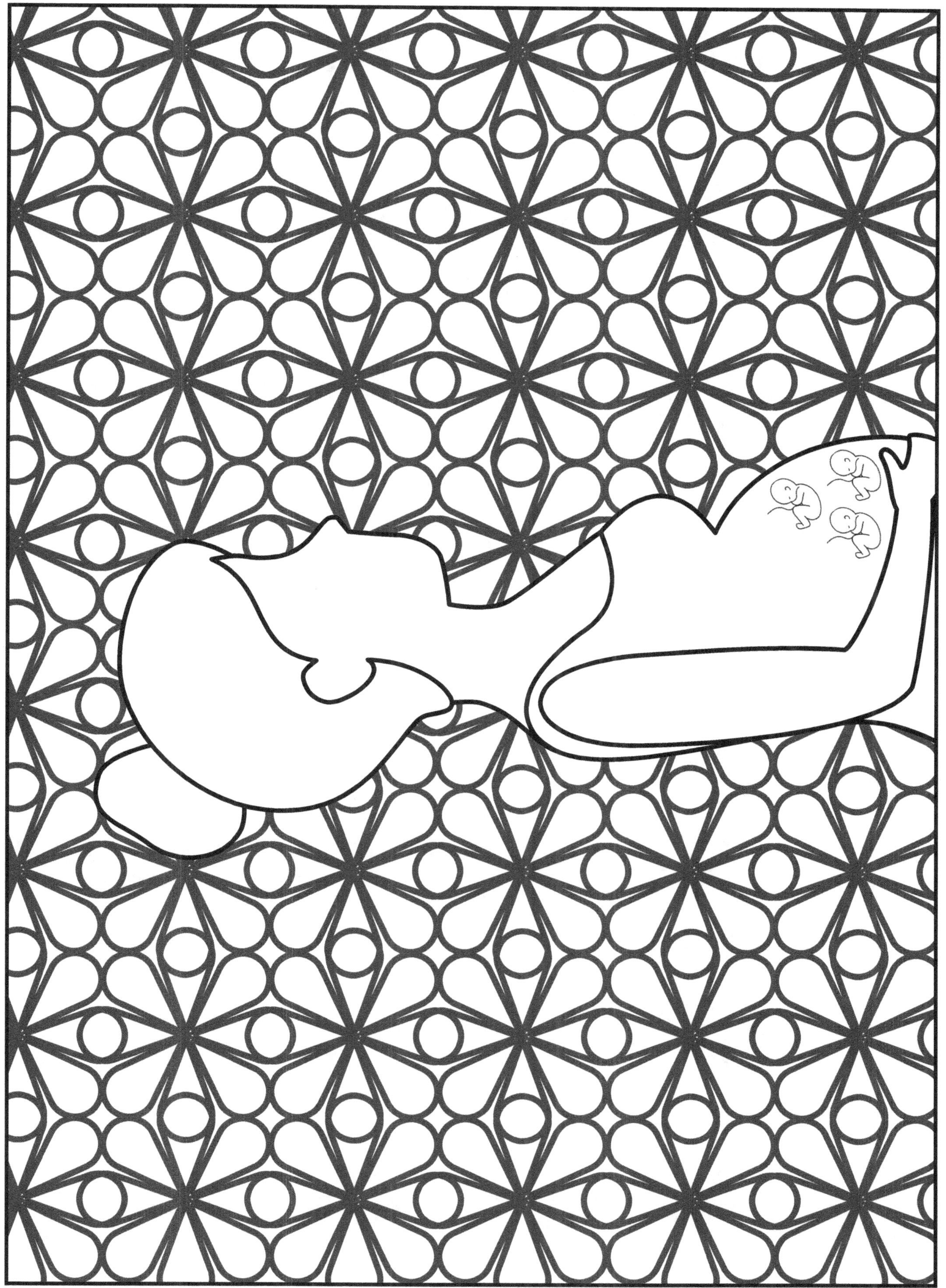

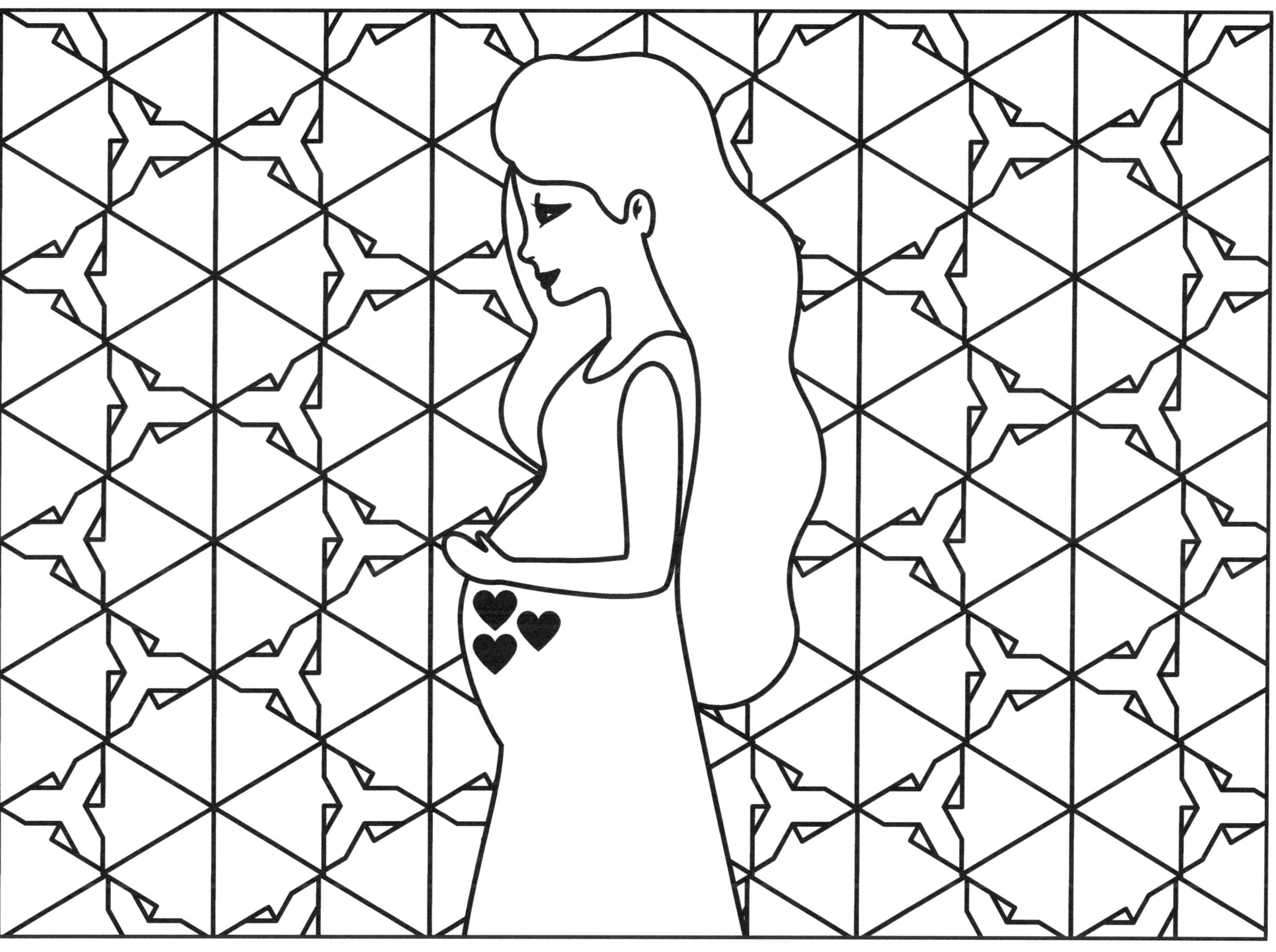

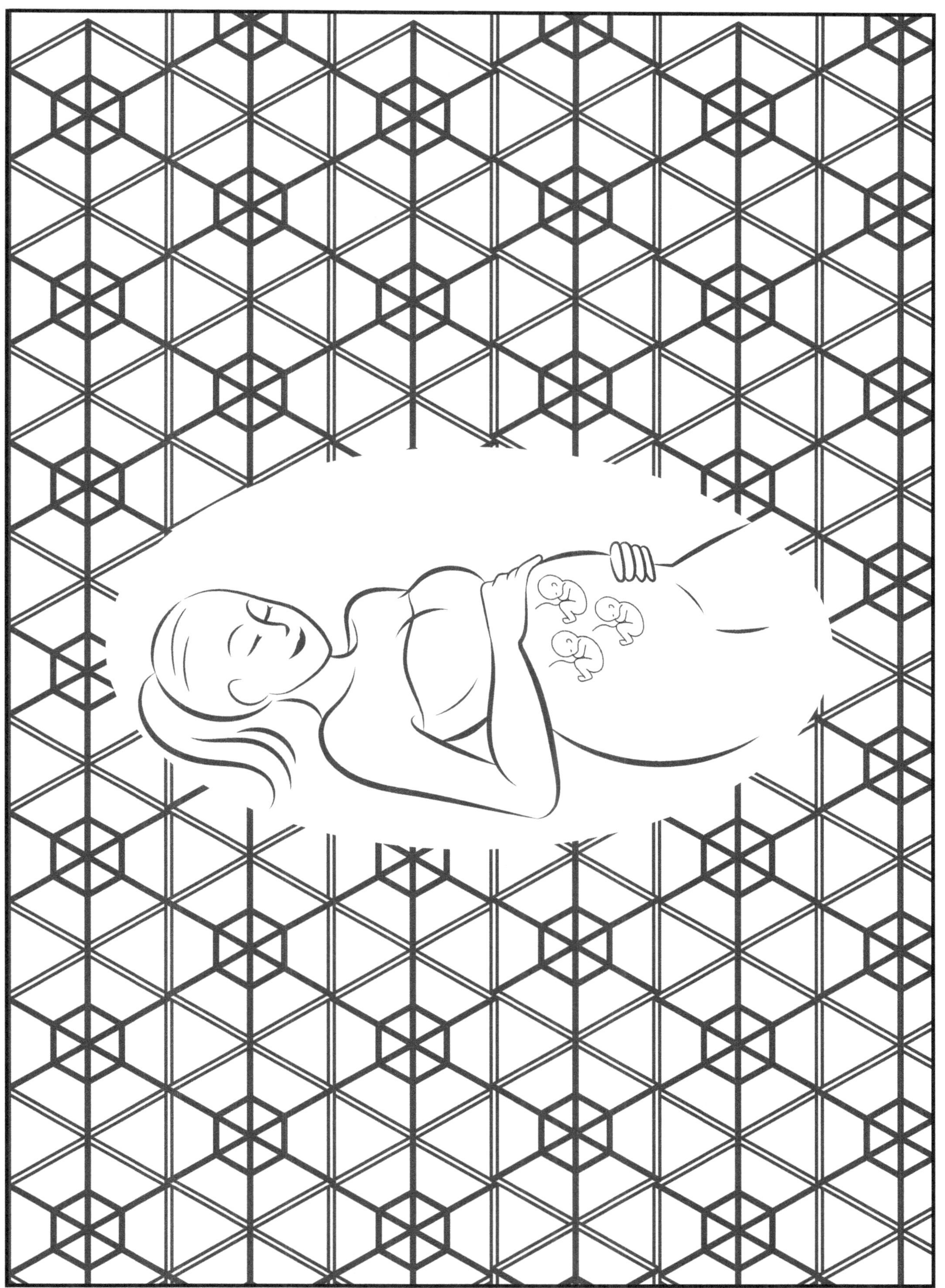

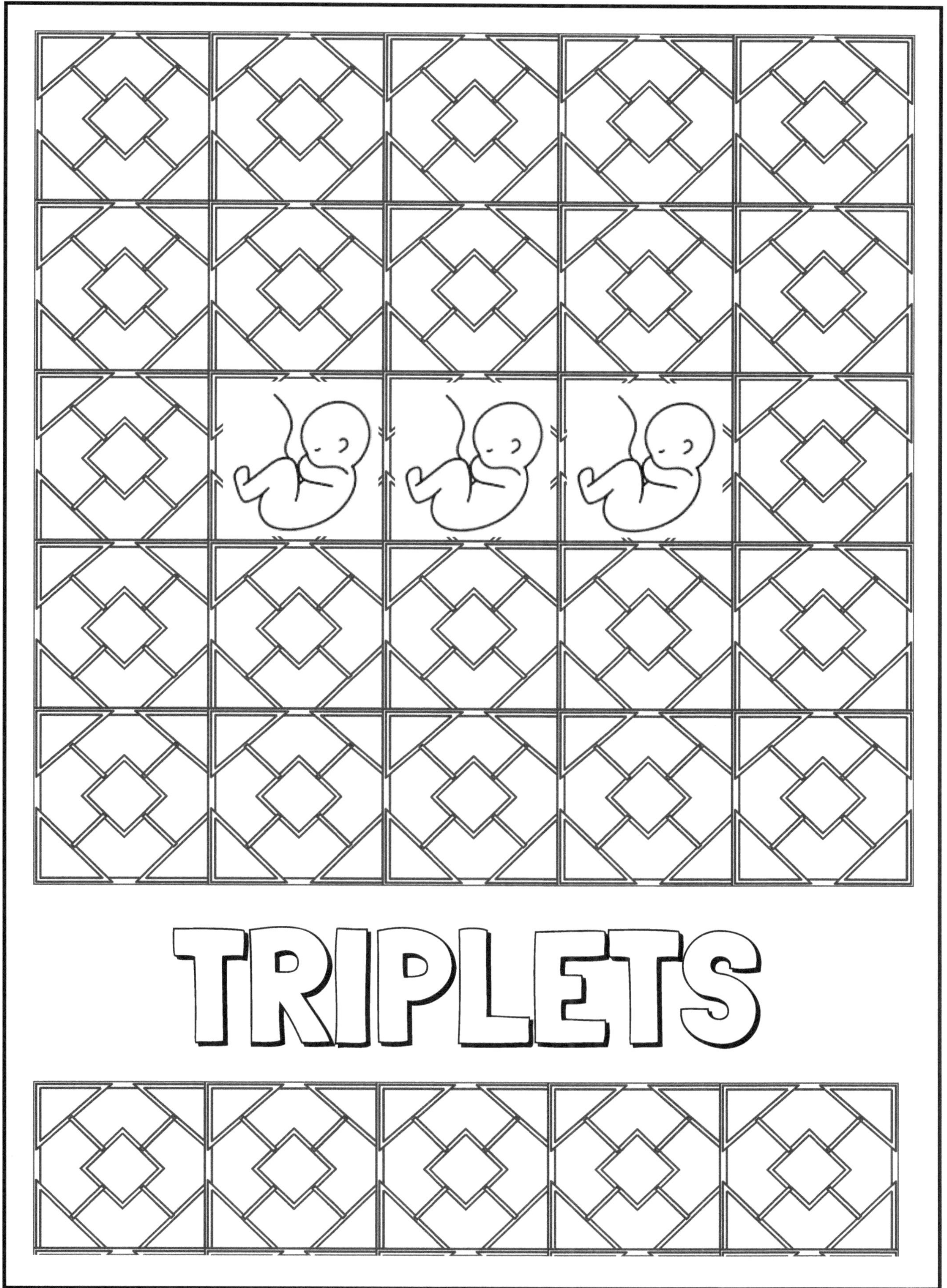
TRIPLETS

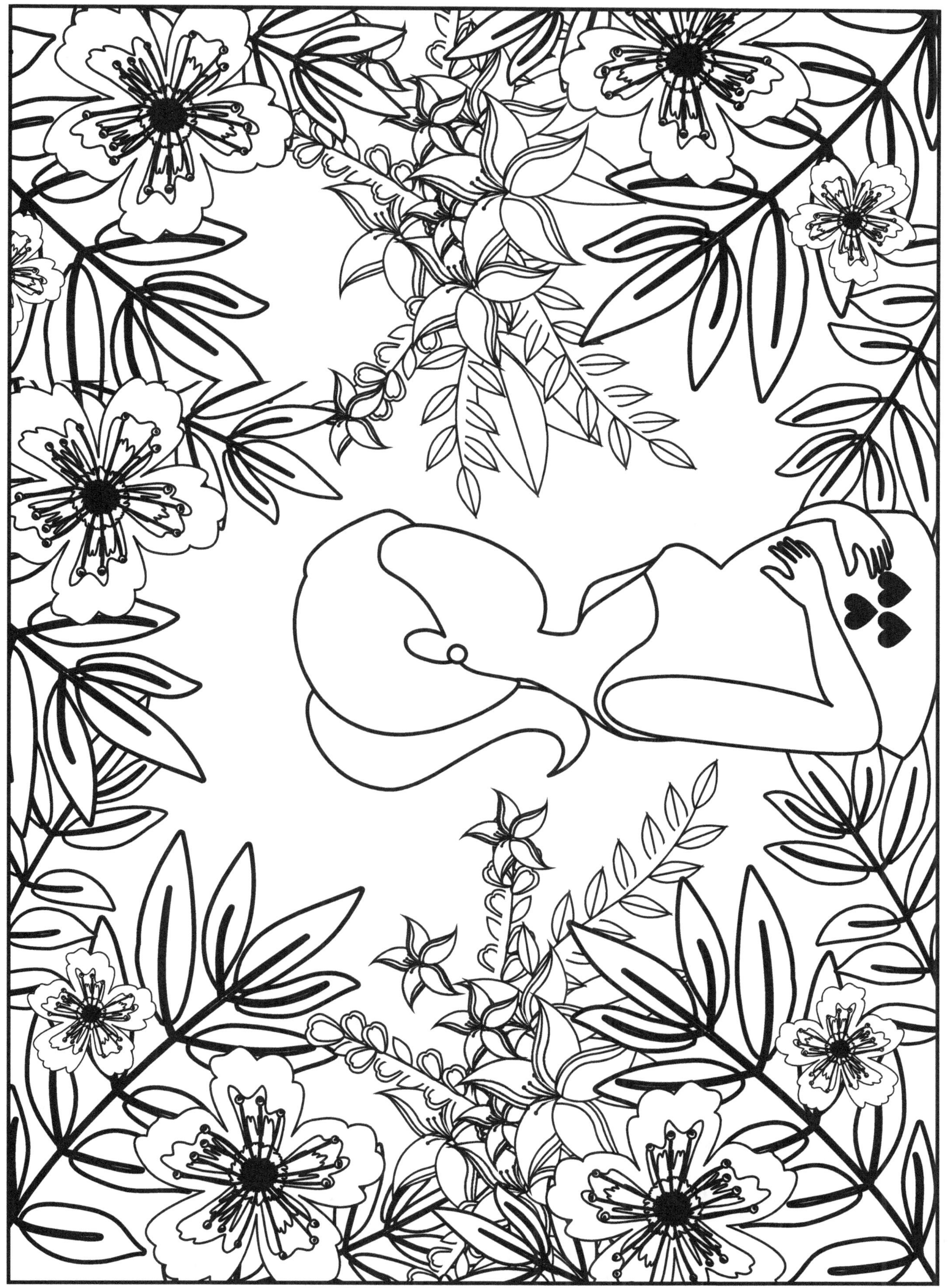

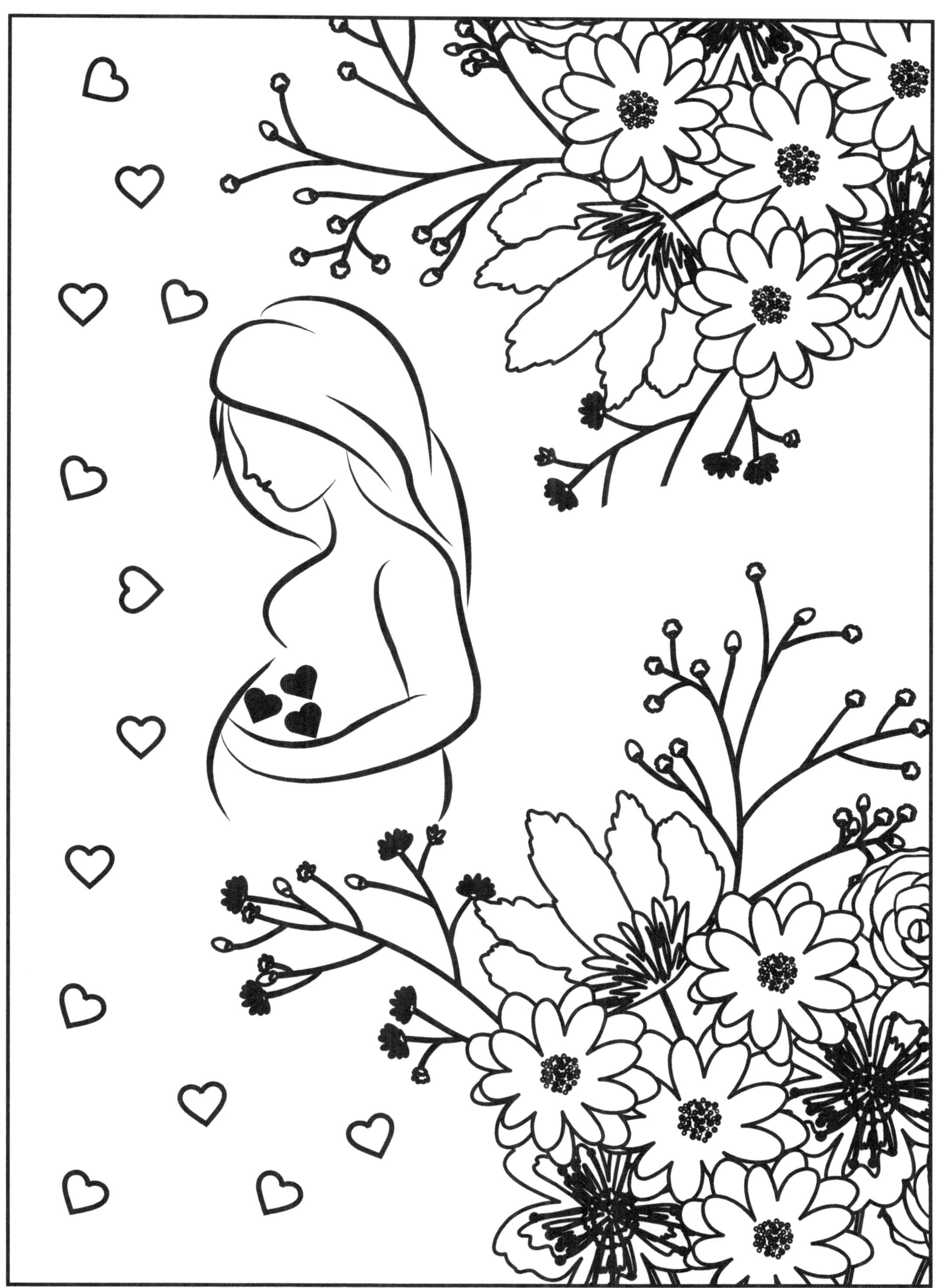

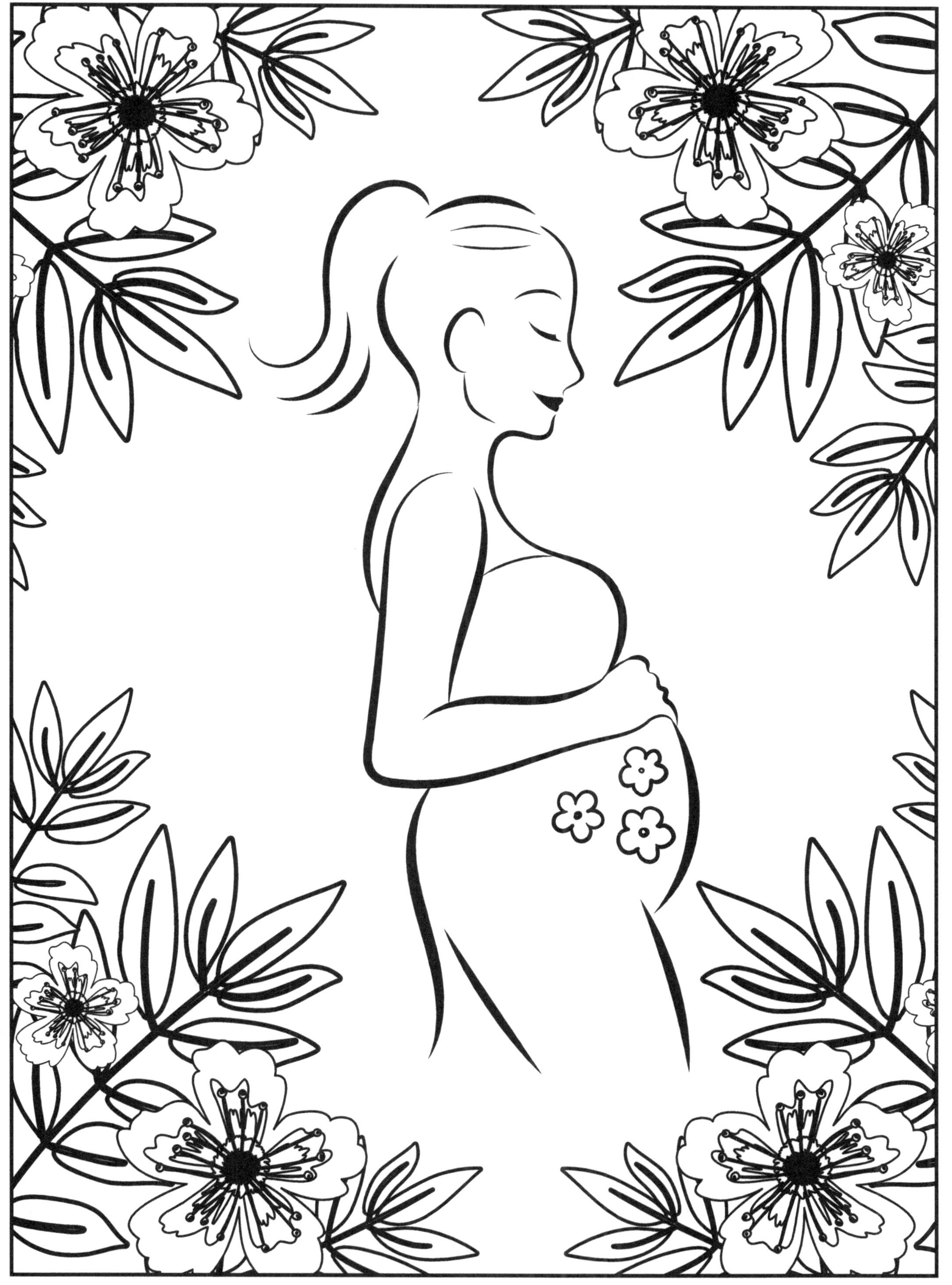

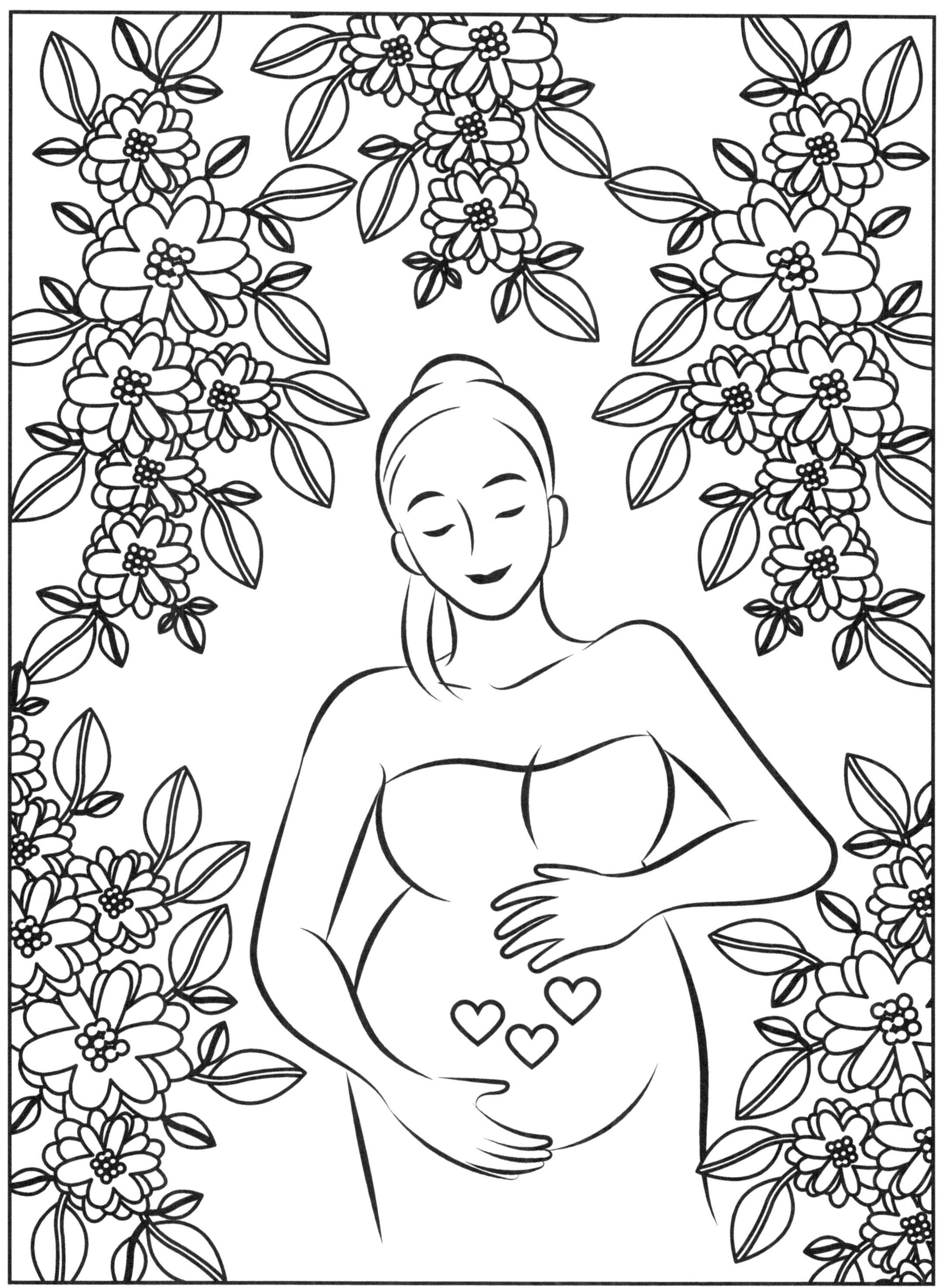

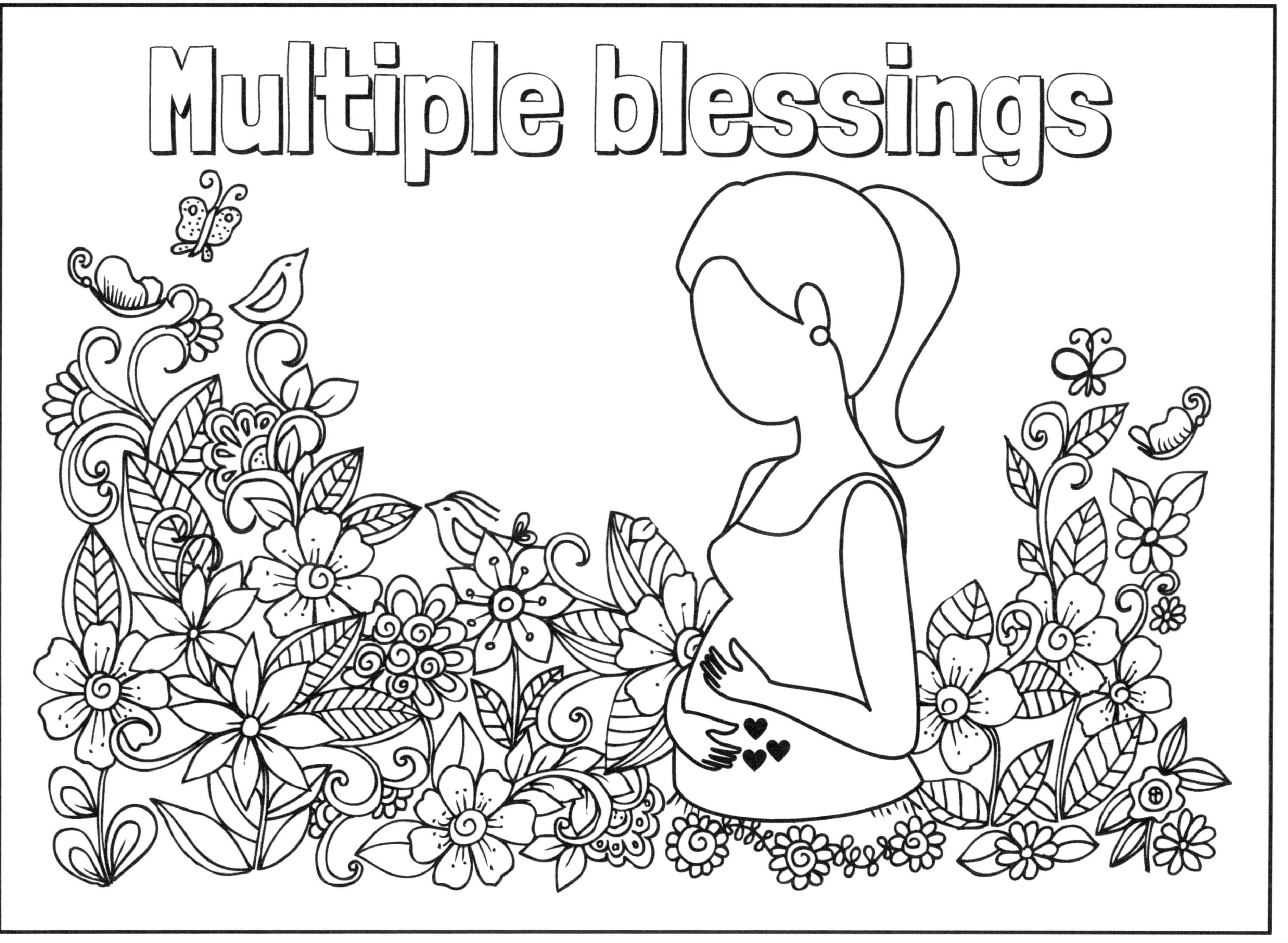

Multiple blessings

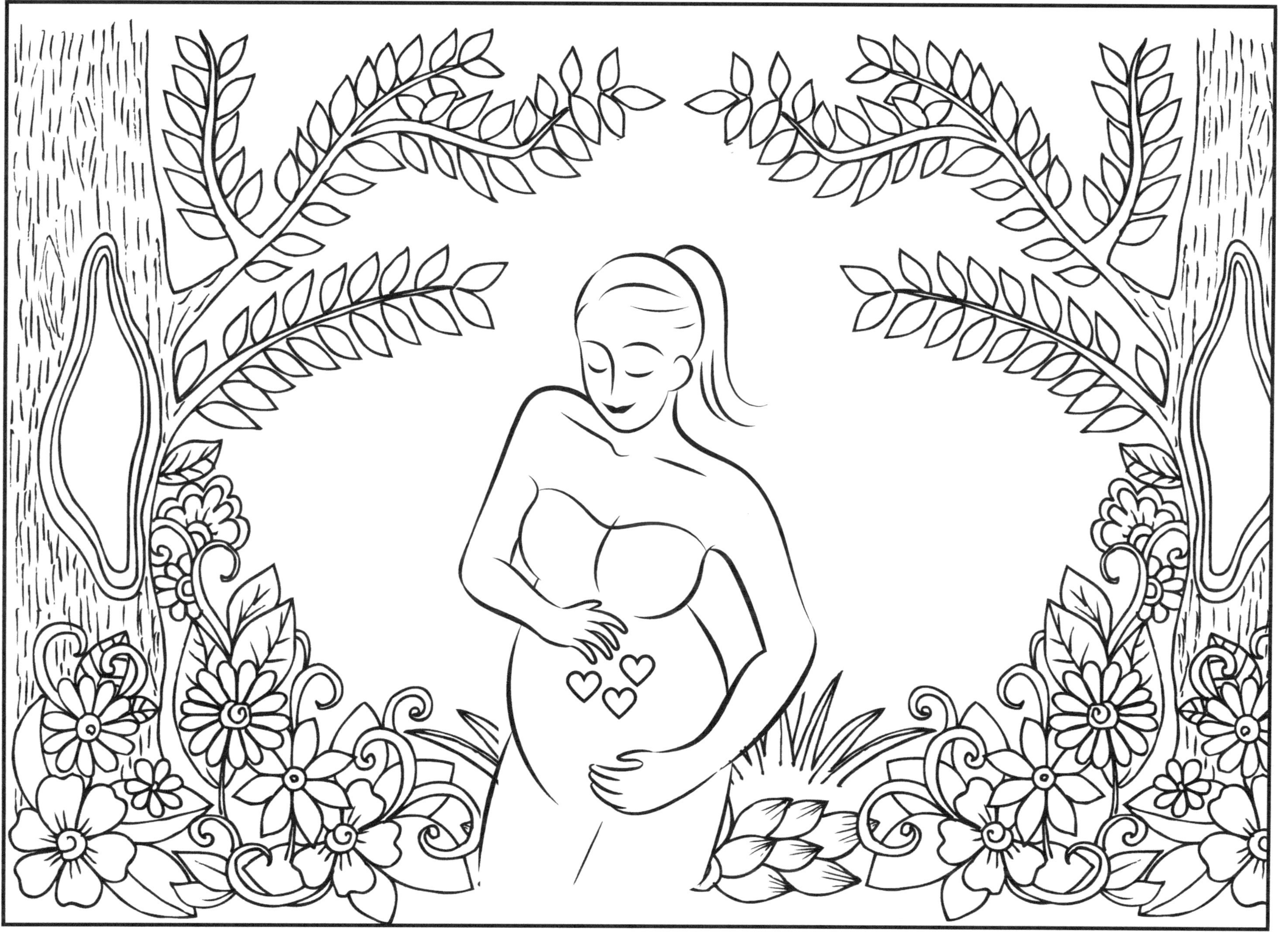

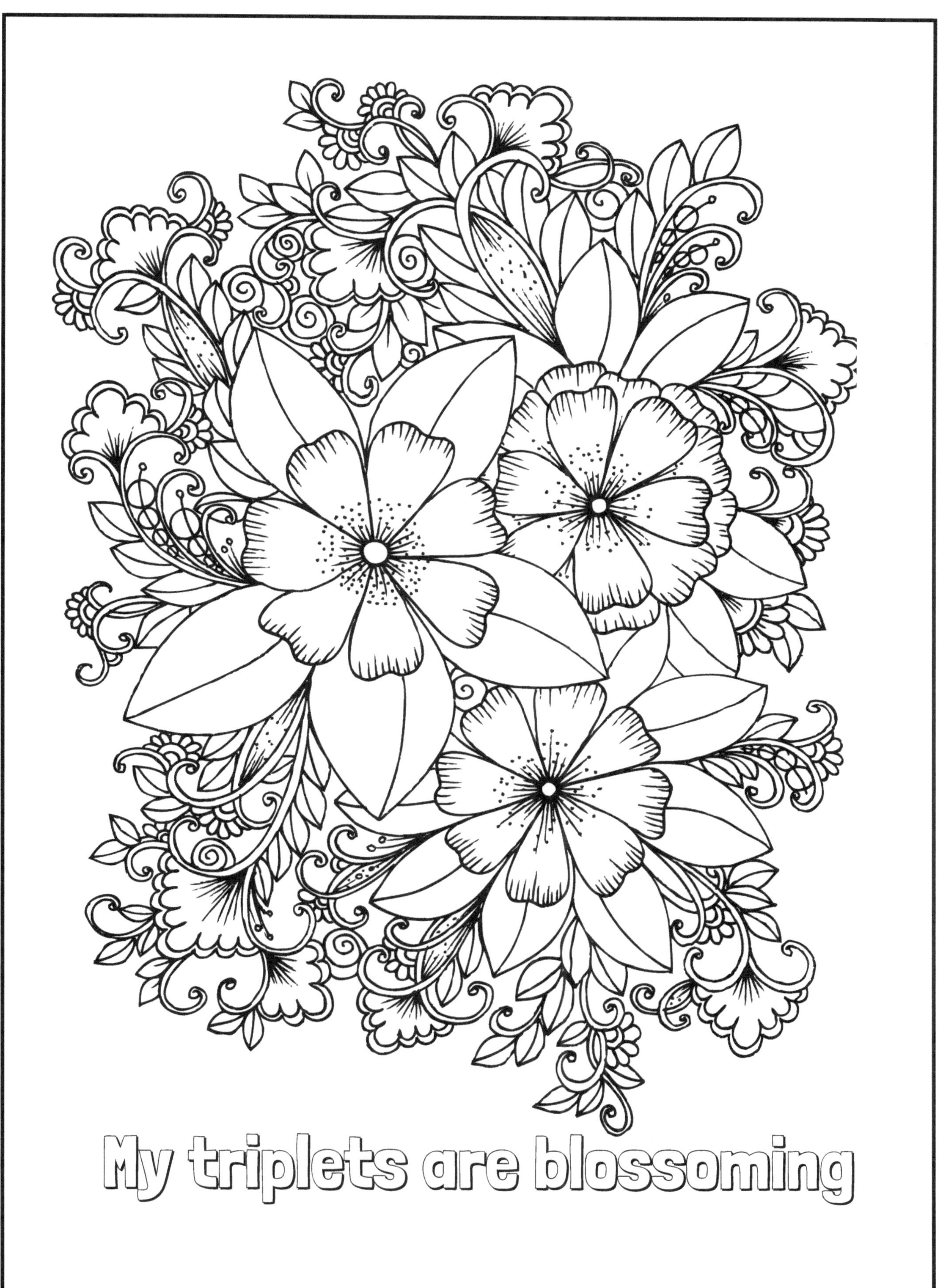

My triplets are blossoming

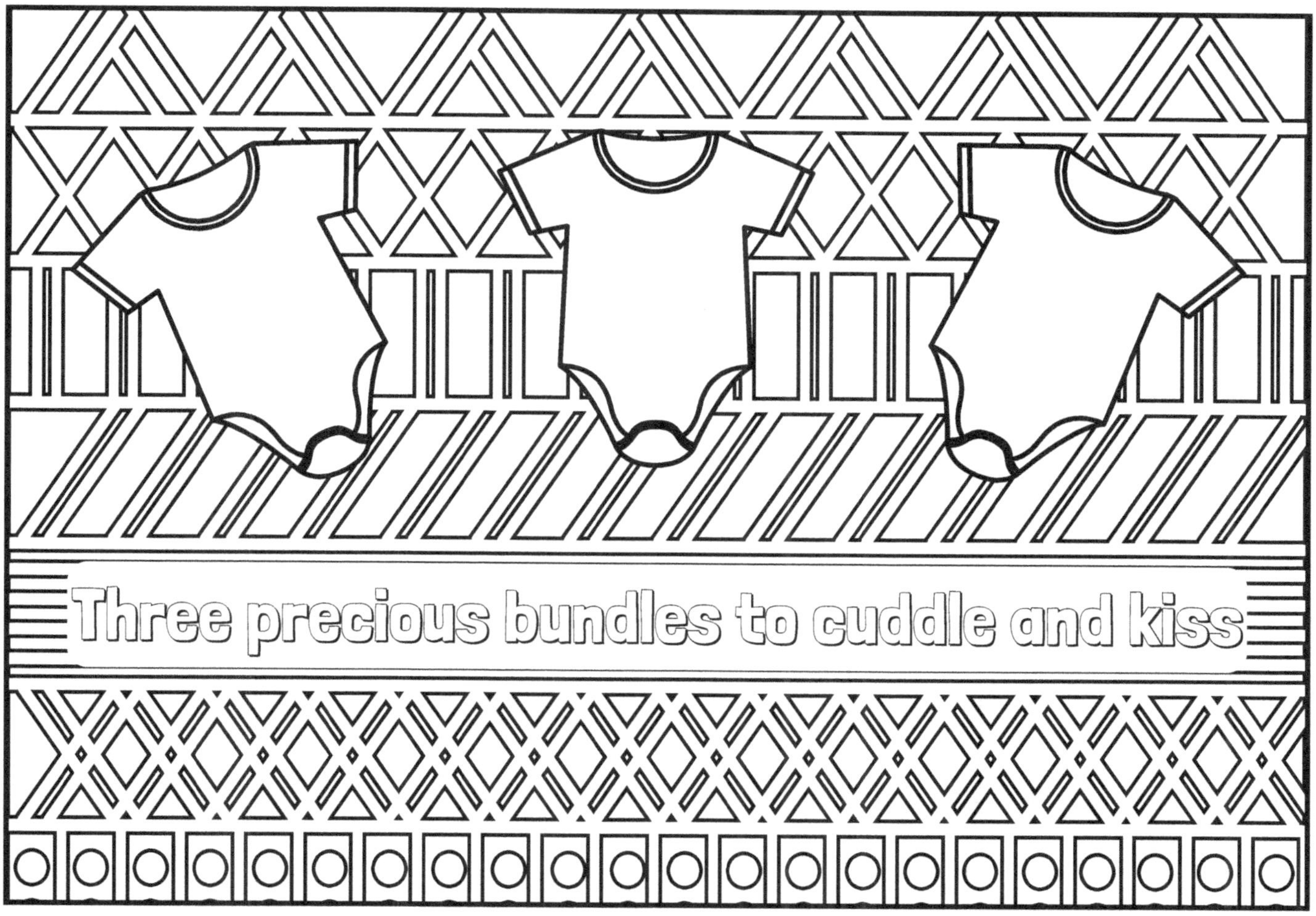

Three precious bundles to cuddle and kiss

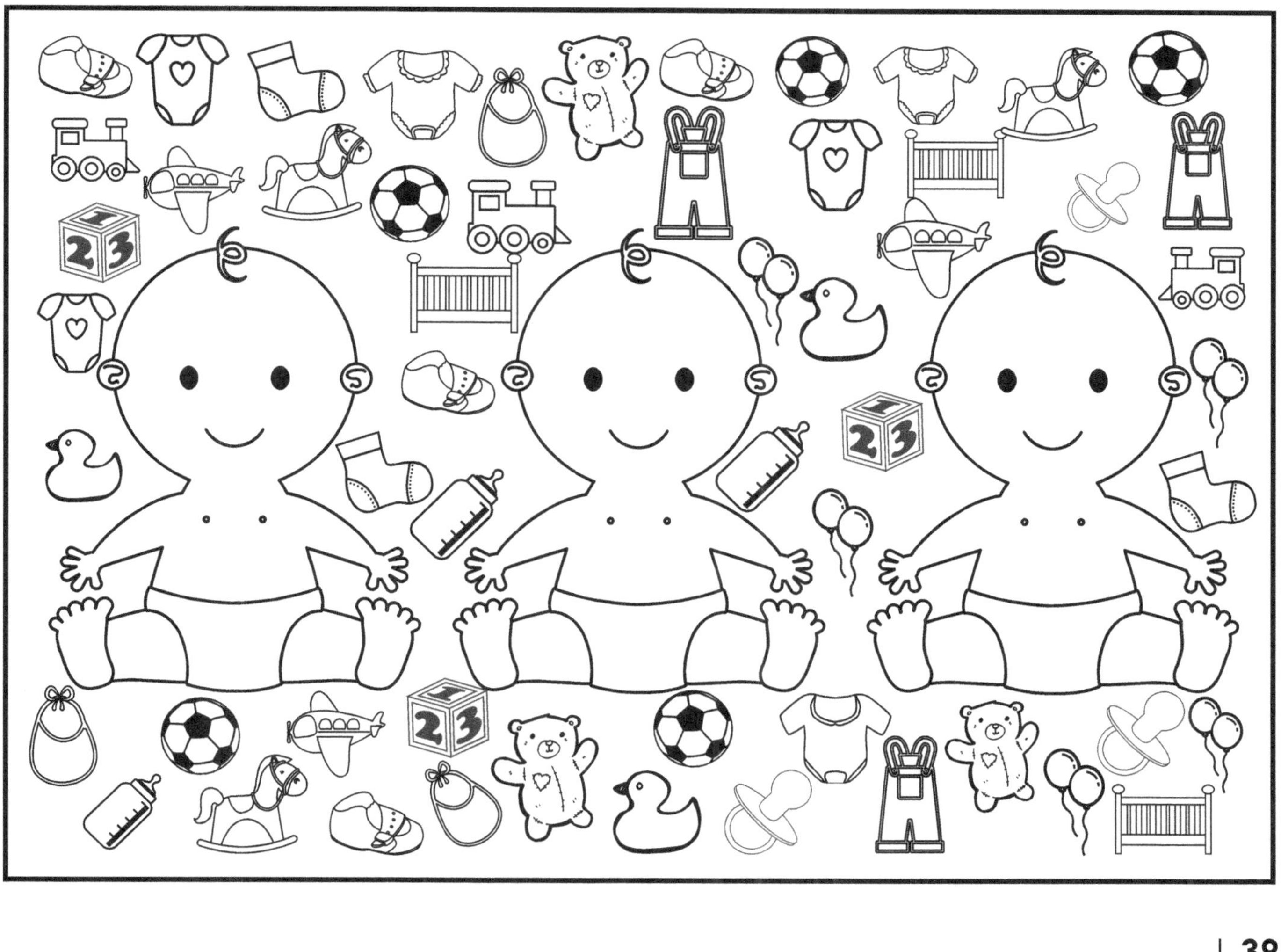

Three to love

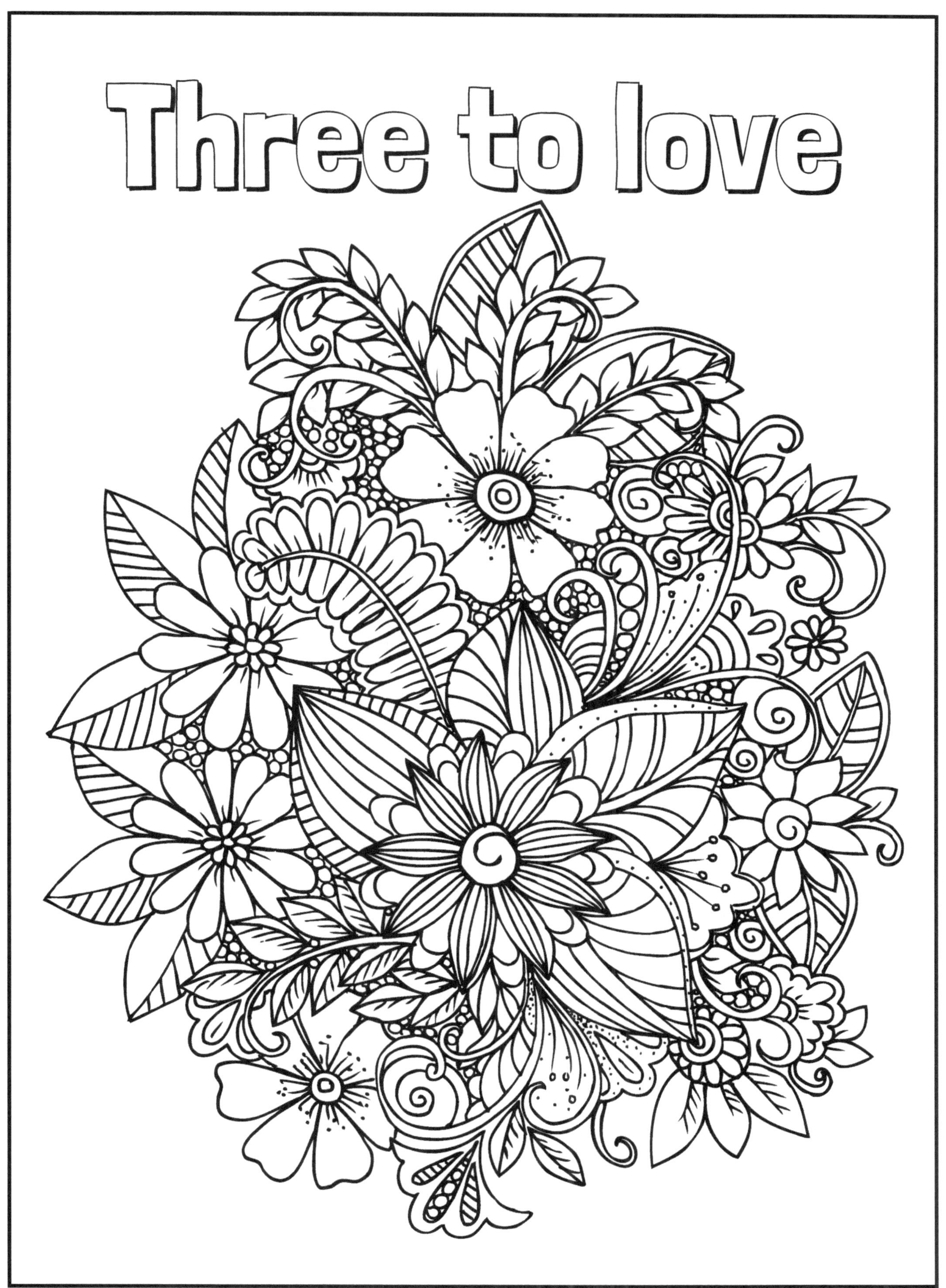

Triple
blessings

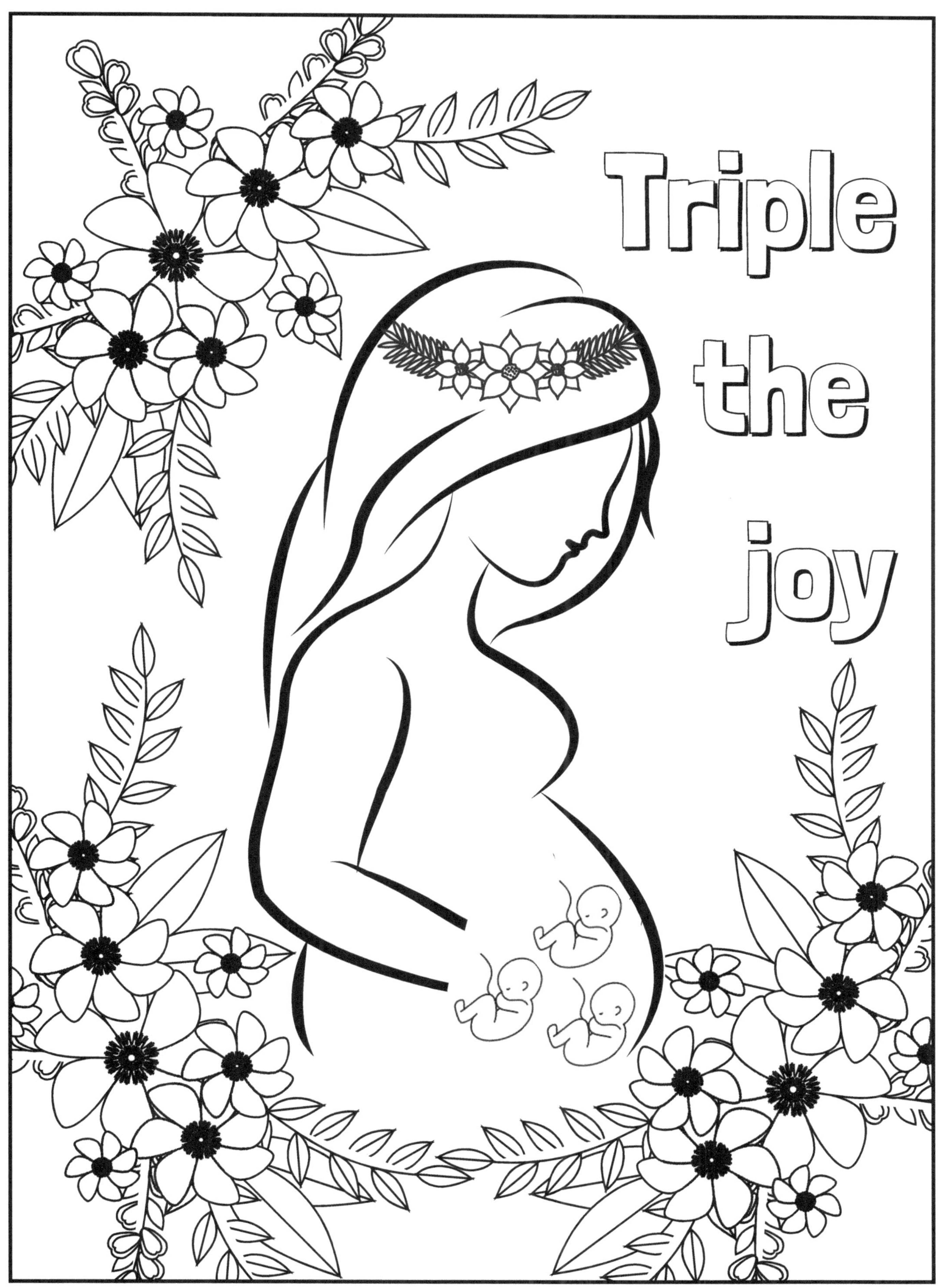

Triple
the
joy

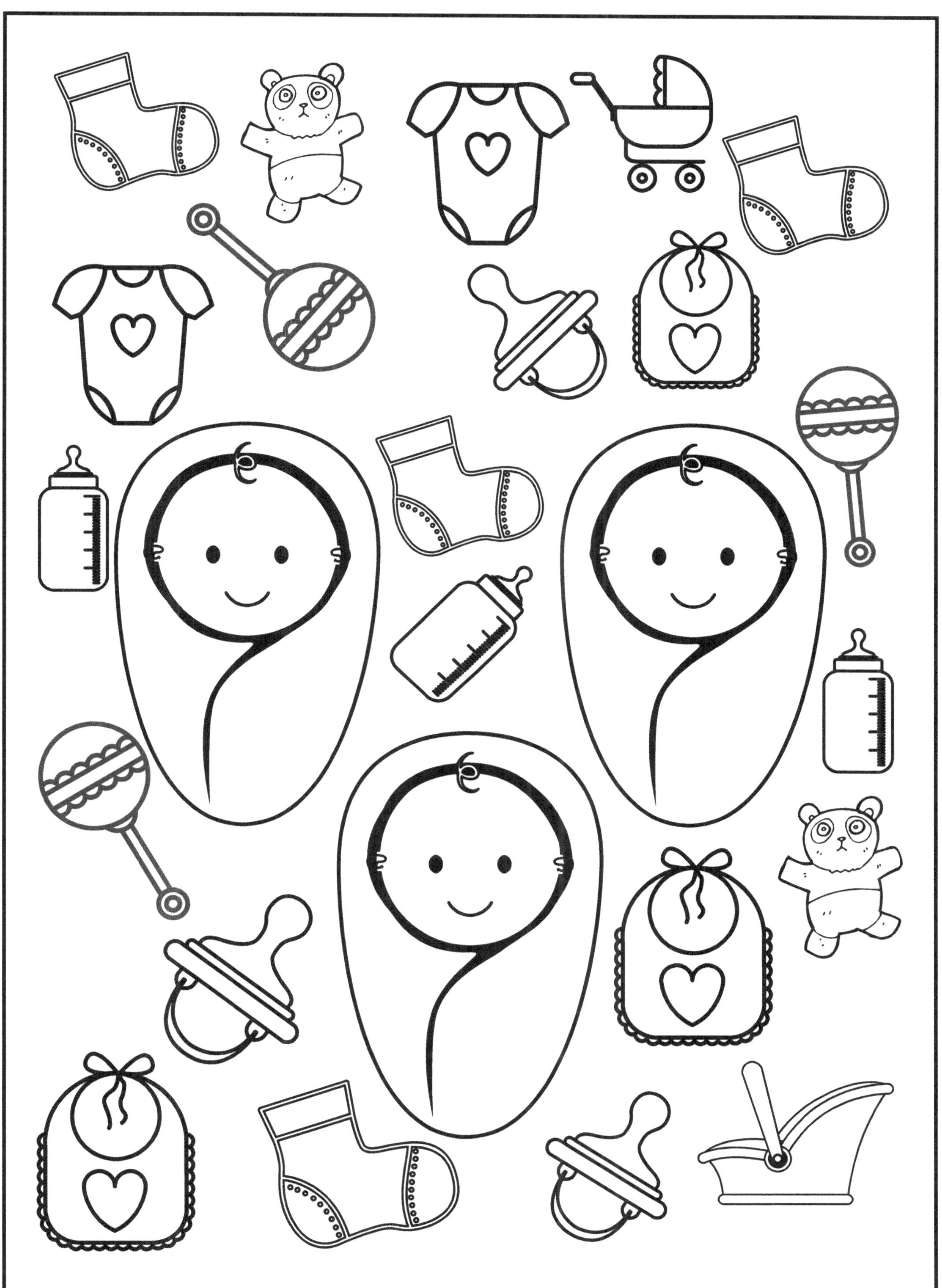

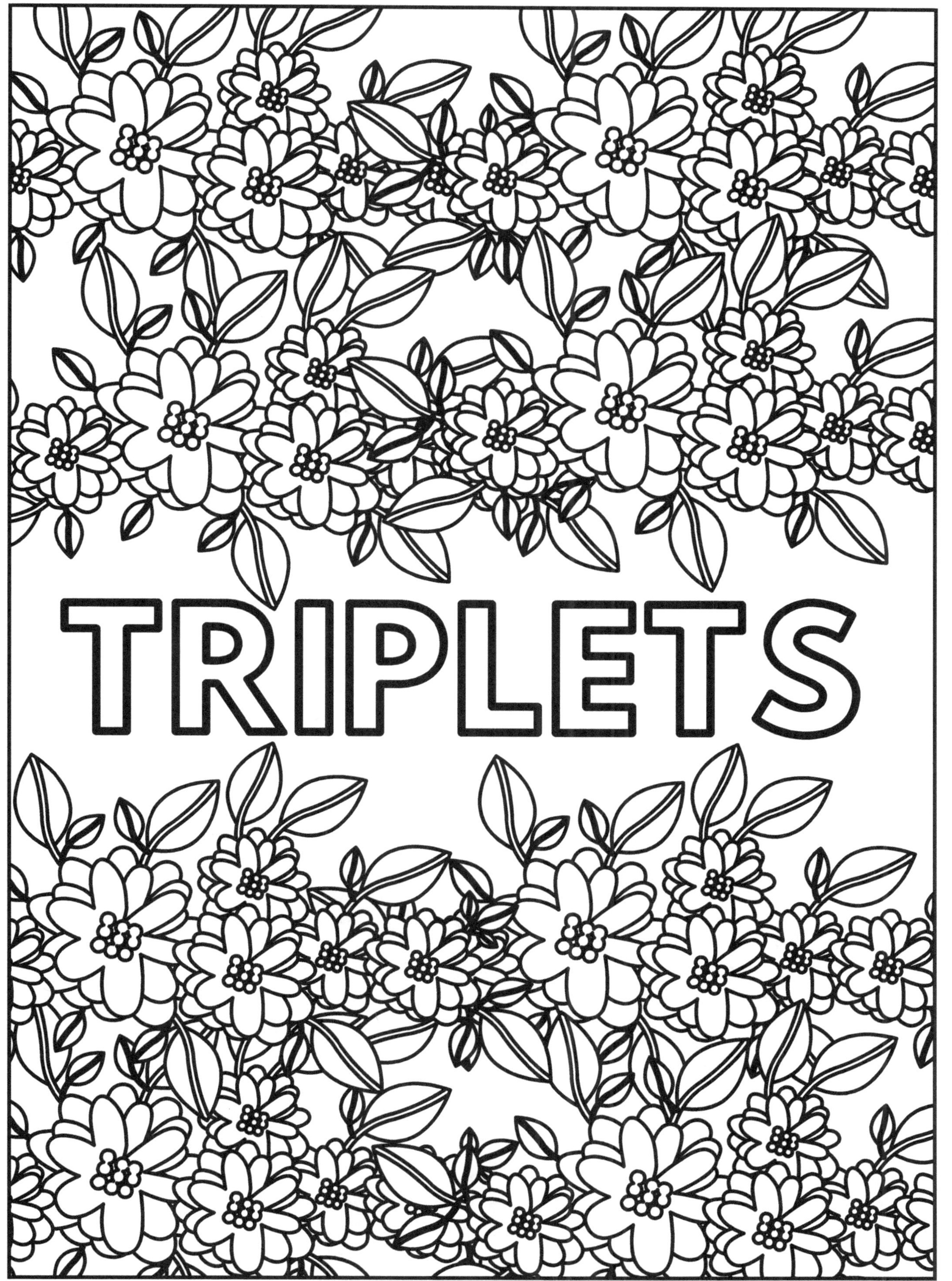
TRIPLETS

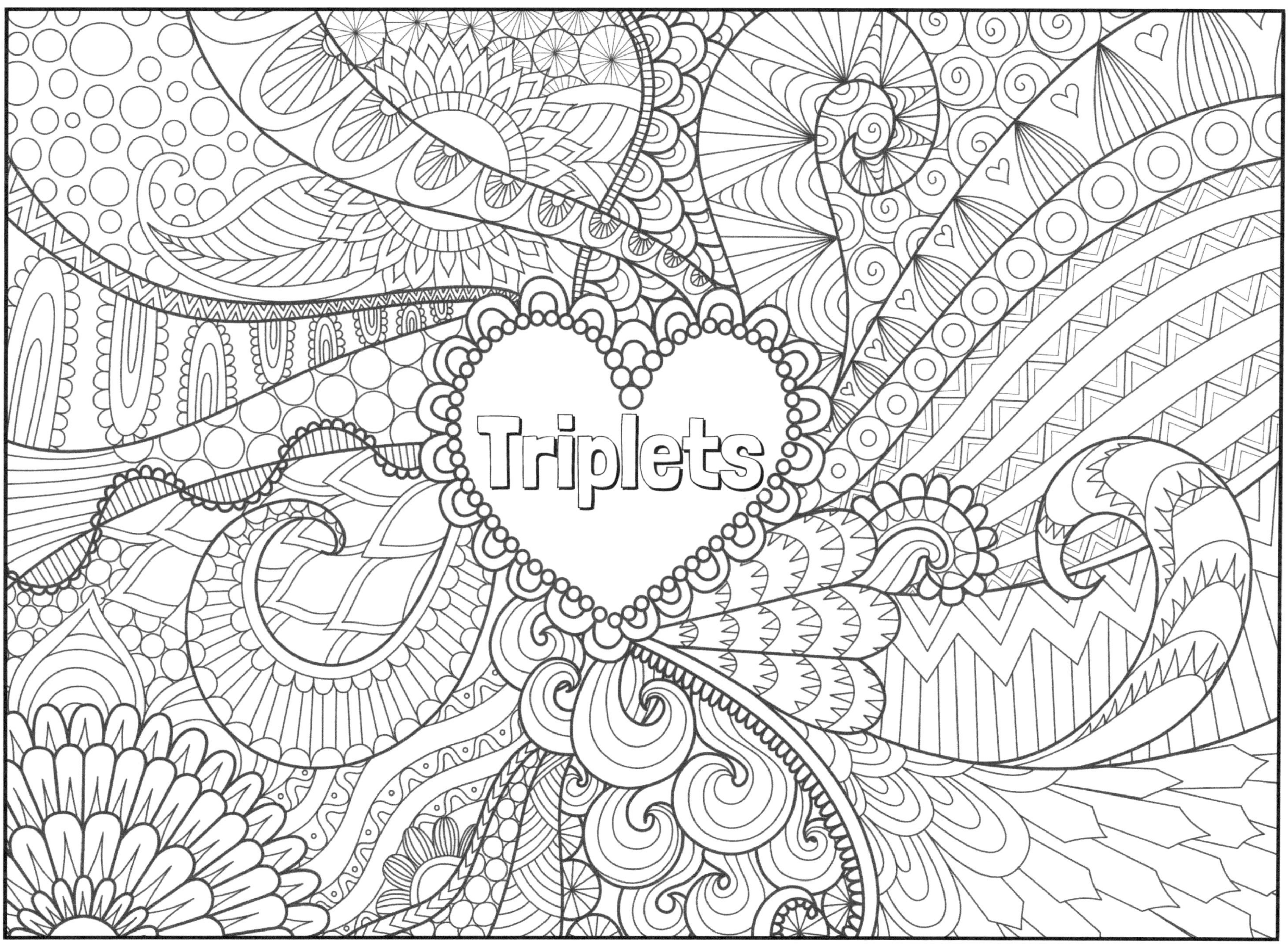
Triplets

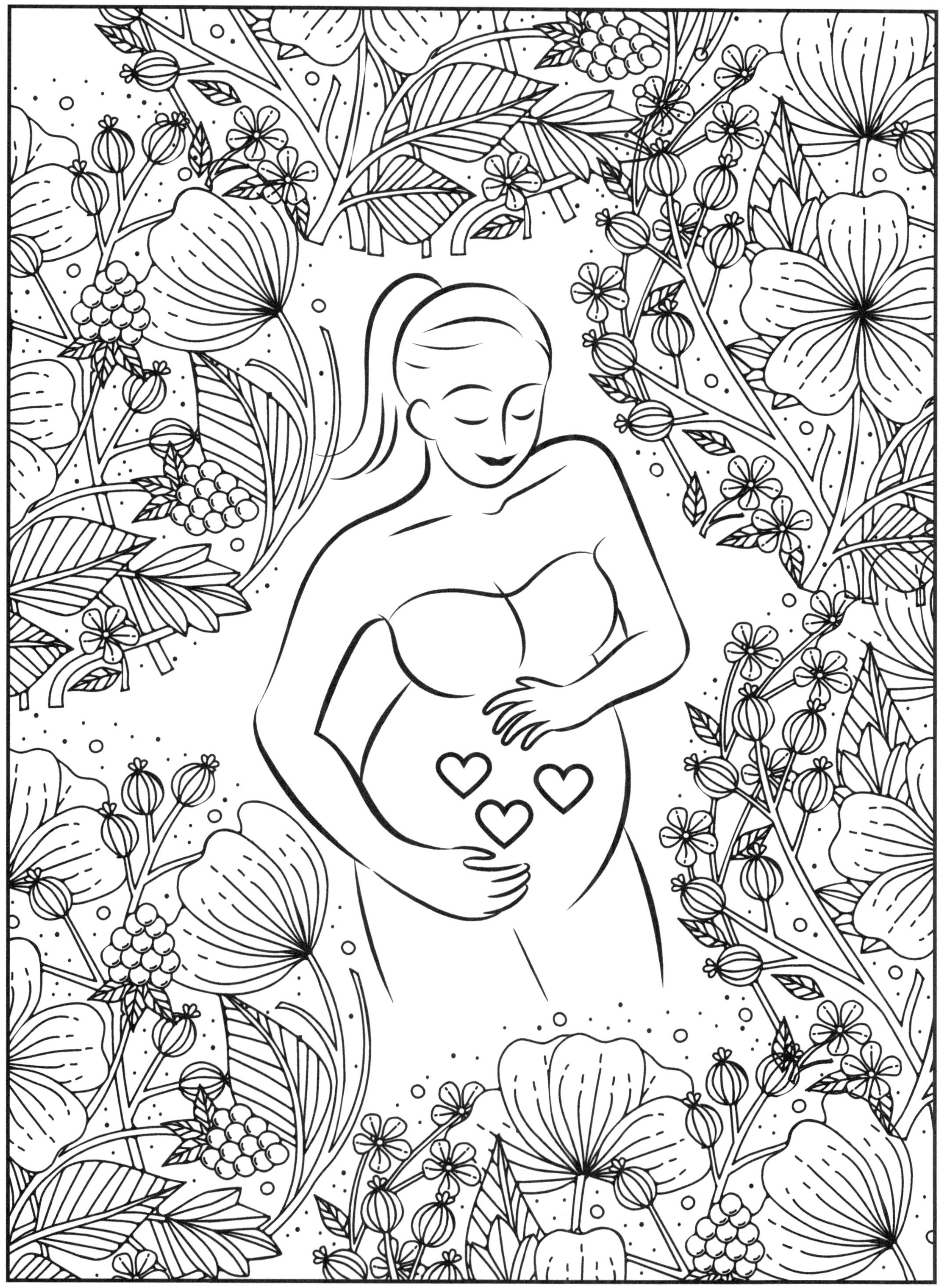

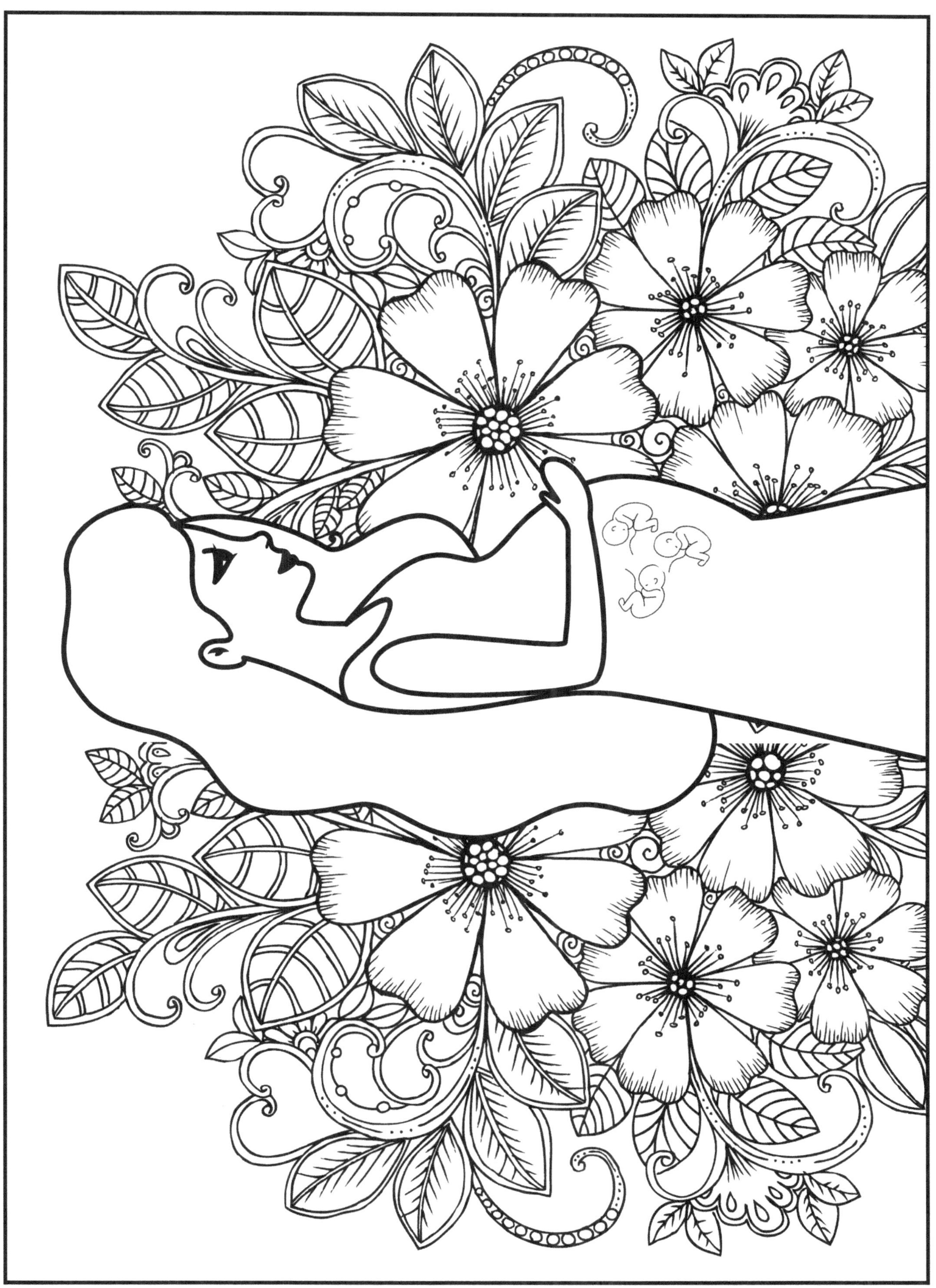

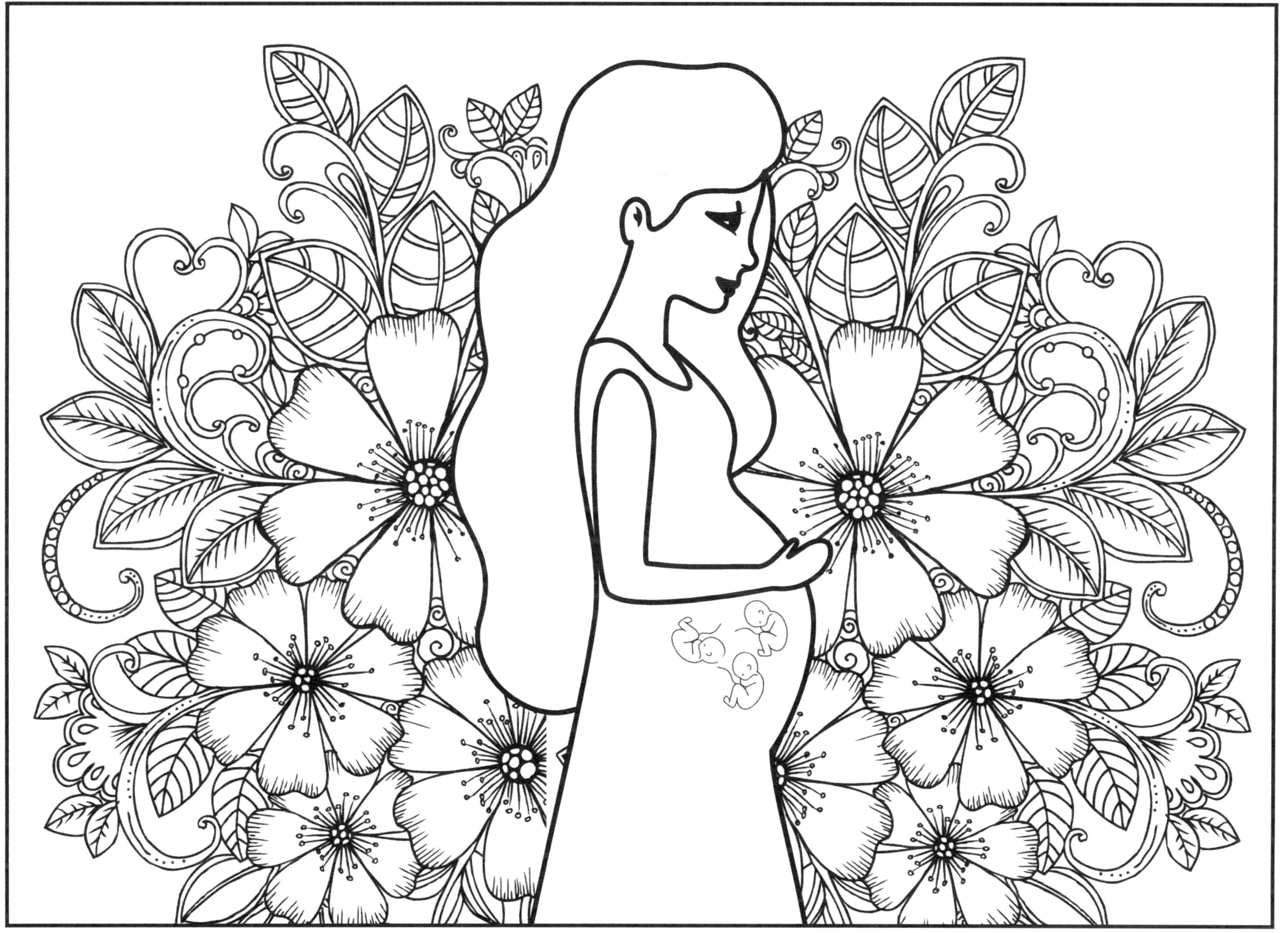

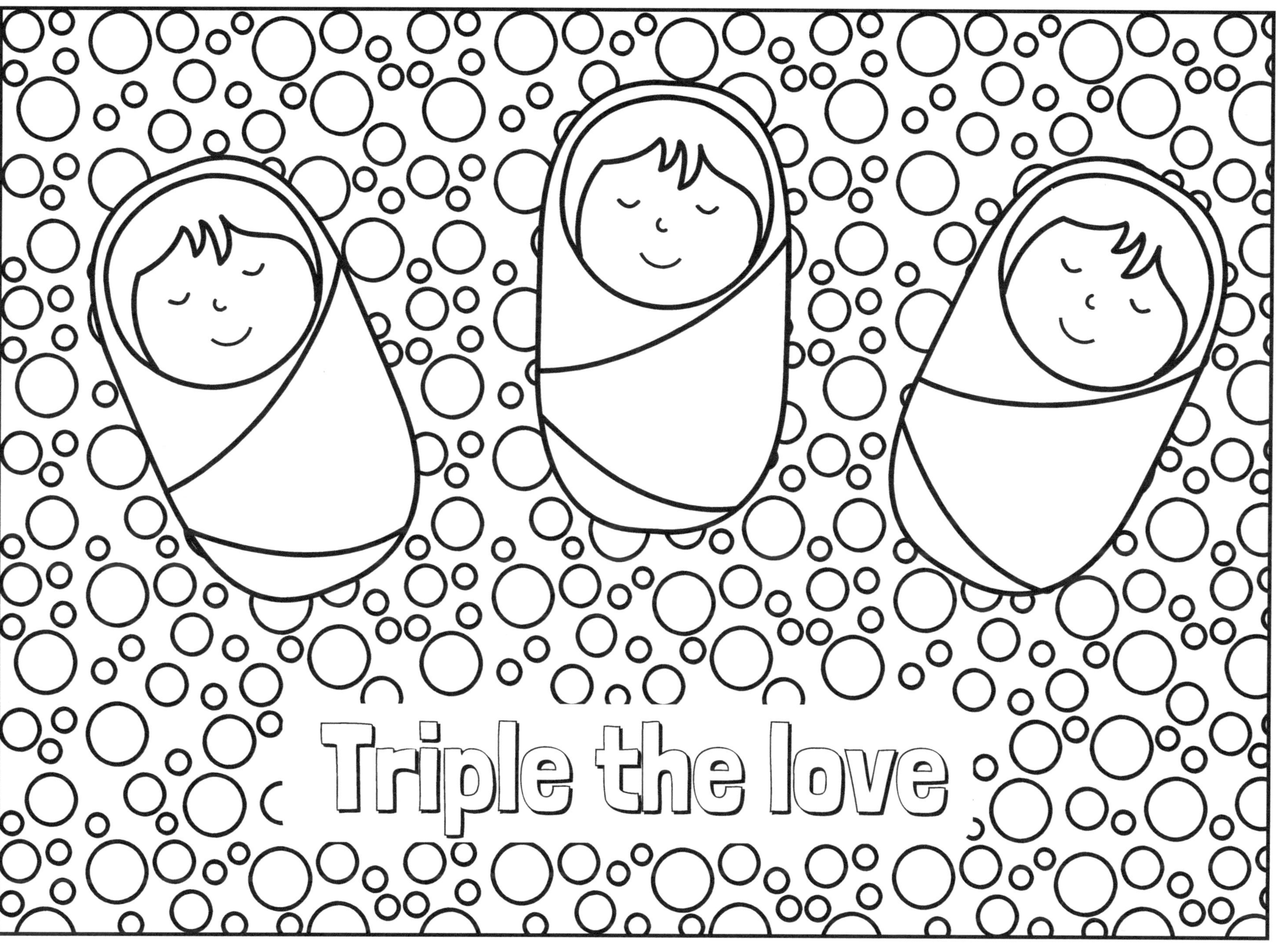

Triple the love